VERSAILLES

VISITOR'S GUIDE

TEXT

Béatrix Saule and Daniel Meyer
Head Curators

Editorial co-ordination: Denis Kilian (Director, Éditions Art Lys)
Editorial follow-up and picture research: Christian Ryo
Layout: Martine Mène
Plans: Thierry Lebreton, Dominique Bissière
Production: Pierre Kegels

© Éditions Art Lys
4, rue Saint-Fiacre
78000 Versailles

ISBN 2-85495-117-4

CONTENTS

The Versailles Estate

With its three châteaux, gardens, park and annexes, Versailles is an immense estate. Although Louis XIII had a hunting-lodge and garden built there, it was Louis XIV who was the true creative force. He turned Versailles into a sumptuous estate and ensured its destiny. From 1682 to 1789, Versailles was the seat and later the symbol of absolute monarchy, since the estate, modelled according to the Sun King's wishes, reflected his perception of power.

For the service of the King and his magnificence

Not too close to Paris, where insurgency was always a threat, but not too far away, the site had great potential for building. It thus fulfilled the King's desire to have his court permanently around him, which no other royal residence in the surrounding areas permitted. At the expense of considerable building work, decorating and excavation work, and laying on water, everything was created for the service of the King, his pleasure and his magnificence: the town, the annexes – including the stables, the Grand Commun for the lodgings of the officers of the royal house, the wings for the ministers, the château with its public and private apartments, the gardens for walking, the small park and, beyond, the large park for hunting… Furthermore, everything was ordered around a main axis passing through the very centre of the royal dwelling, where the King's Bedchamber was located from 1701.

The estate today

Three centuries after it was created, the estate is still vast despite losing its hunting grounds. The figures testify to this: 800 hectares, 20 km of roads, as many enclosing walls, 200,000 trees and more flowers planted each year, 35 km of canalisation, 11 hectares of roofing, 2153 windows, 700 rooms, 67 staircases, etc.
It retains from its origin J. Hardouin-Mansart's noble architecture, both at Versailles and the Grand Trianon, the regular layout of Le Nôtre's gardens and exotic groves, an abundance of statues making it the largest open-air sculpture museum in the world, and its sparkling fountains still functioning as of old. Although the interiors of the château have seen more changes with time, the 18th Century left its imprint of elegance and nature on the estate: the Petit Trianon, built by Gabriel by order of Louis XV and, under Louis XVI, the Grove of the Baths of Apollo, designed by Hubert Robert, and the Queen's Hamlet, so revealing of Marie-Antoinette's personality.
We invite you to take time to discover all the riches of Versailles, bathed in so much history, which we are attempting to safeguard, restore to life and share with you.

I have returned from Versailles.
I have seen the beautiful apartments;
They are enchanting. If I had read about it in a story,
I would have built a château in Spain
to see its true nature.
I have beheld and touched it; it is truly delightful.
MADAME DE SÉVIGNÉ

It is not a palace,
it is a whole town
Magnificent in scale,
magnificent in substance.
CHARLES PERRAULT

It is a château that may be called
an enchanted palace,
since the artistic adjustments
have so effectively helped
nature's efforts in perfecting it.
MOLIÈRE

THE CHÂTEAUX DE TRIANON

34 The Grand Trianon
35 The Petit Trianon
36 The French Pavilion
37 The Belvedere
38 The Temple of Love
39 The Great Lake
40 The Queen's Cottage
41 The Mill
42 The Farm

THE AVENUES AND GROVES

To the north

17 The Fountain of Ceres or Summer
18 The Fountain of Flora or Spring
19 The Baths of Apollo
20 The Rond Vert and the Children's Island
21 The North Quincunxes
22 The Bosquet de l'Etoile (Star Grove)
23 The Bosquet des Dômes
24 The Obelisk
25 The Fountain of Enceladus

To the south

26 The Fountain of Bacchus or Autumn
27 The Fountain of Saturn or Winter
28 The Ballroom or Bosquet de Rocailles
29 The Queen's Grove
30 The South Quincunxes
31 The King's Garden
32 The Colonnade
33 The Salle des Marronniers

The Stables and the Coach Museum

Located in the twin buildings facing the château, the Great and Small Stables fulfilled two different and often rival functions. In the Great Stables, overseen by the Master of the Horse, some 300 horses were trained for war or for hunting. The Small Stables, administered by the First Equerry, were responsible for the carriages, carriage teams and ordinary mounts. The buildings house the riding-schools, staff quarters and the school for the pages. They were built rapidly in 1680, under the supervision of J. Hardouin-Mansart. Due to their vastness, magnificent architecture and sumptuous sculptural décor, it was rumoured that the King of France's horses had more lavish lodgings than the Princes of Europe! Louis XIV was very proud of the Stables and freely welcomed visitors.

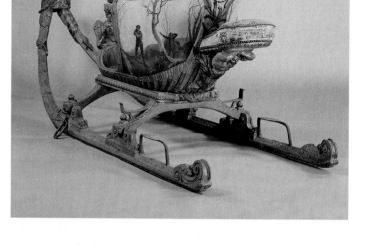

During the winter, the Court was entertained by sleigh rides or races through the snow-covered avenues of the park.

Sedan chairs were widely used within the château for crossing the courtyards and also the long inner galleries. There were private chairs and royal sedan chairs which were rented at a price of 6 sols per day.

The Coach Museum occupies a gallery in the Great Stables, which has been preserved, with its mangers and fodder racks, as in the time of Louis XIV. Since the 2000 carriages used by the Court were sold during the Revolution, it was Louis-Philippe who assembled the sleighs, sedan chairs and berlins which make up the current collection. The berlins, commissioned in celebration of dynastic events (marriages, christenings, coronations, and funerals) by Napoleon I, Louis XVIII and Charles X, are exceptionally sumptuous, particularly the Coronation Coach of Charles X.

The Courtyards and Façades, town side

Beyond the Place d'Armes, situated below the gateway, stand several disparate buildings, extending both in length and breadth, evoking an image of a town more than a château. From this side, there is very little in common with the majestic linearity of the façades overlooking the park. Behind the gateway, there is a succession of narrowing courtyards: the Great Courtyard, Royal Courtyard and Marble Courtyard. The buildings follow the brick, stone and slate architecture of the first Château of Versailles built by Louis XIII, which Louis XIV wanted to preserve. Later on, the architects always intended to rework the façades, aiming to make them higher, with a more noble style and material. It is in the same spirit that Hardouin-Mansart designed the Royal Chapel, and Gabriel built the wing and colonnaded pavilion which bear his name nearby.

When Pierre-Denis Martin painted this view, the buildings showed the same blue-white-red harmony. A second set of railings, destroyed during the Revolution, enclosed the Royal Courtyard, marking off "the King's Dwelling".

Under Louis XIV, the clock in the Marble Courtyard governed the life of the court; but, after the death of the King, its hands were symbolically stopped.

Now the centre of an immense château, the small château built by Louis XIII needed to be improved. Louis XIV embellished it with marble paving, an ornamental front with a projection and columns, and masses of sculptures.

The village of Versailles was first noticed by Henri IV and then his son Louis XIII because of its woods abounding in game. Louis XIII acquired a hunting-lodge there in 1624, which he replaced in 1631 with a small château, built by Philibert Leroy, and found among the buildings surrounding the present Marble Courtyard.

However, it was Louis XIV who gave Versailles its renown. When the personal reign of the Sun King began in 1661 after the death of Cardinal Mazarin, the major work was also initiated. In two years, the King spent no less than one million five hundred thousand livres divided between extension of the park, reconstruction of the buildings in the Great Courtyard (the present old wing), and embellishment of the apartments, which had until then been very plain. From then on, as shown in the paintings by Pierre Patel (1668) and later Pierre-Denis Martin (1722), Versailles gradually took on the proportions and appearance that we see today. The different phases of the work ordered by Louis XIV correspond to the changes in the life of the King and, perhaps, his passions.

From 1668 to 1710, which saw the inauguration of the Royal Chapel, the last building dating from the reign of Louis XIV, Versailles was in a permanent phase of construction. Le Nôtre, who designed the gardens, Le Brun, responsible for the iconography, and Le Vau then Hardouin-Mansart for the architecture, all used their skills to the fullest and transformed a hunting-lodge into a palace renowned throughout the whole world.

In the gardens, the groves would be designed to the rhythm of the lavish festivities at the start of the reign of Louis XIV.

Some of the most remarkable creations have now disappeared, such as the Ambassador's Staircase, destroyed in 1752, and the Bath Apartment. However, the famous Hall of Mirrors still remains; it was completed in 1680, replacing a terrace which separated the King's and Queen's Apartments.

From 1682 to 1789, Versailles was the seat and symbol of the monarchy, apart from a period corresponding to the first few years of the Regency, during which Louis XV resided at Vincennes. Louis XIV's successors did not dramatically transform the general appearance of Versailles; nevertheless, the many alterations to both the gardens and the apartments would finally change the face of the Sun King's dwelling.

Louis XV grew particularly attached to Trianon where he created a new menagerie between 1749 and 1753, the French Pavilion in 1750, and the Petit Trianon in 1761, together with a botanical garden famous the world over, but which would be destroyed by Marie-Antoinette to make room for an English garden and the Queen's Hamlet. In 1770 after the Royal Opera was completed at the end of the north wing, Louis XV resigned himself to the reconstruction of the buildings surrounding the courtyards; however, he died in 1774 before the work could be accomplished, with the exception of the Gabriel Wing, named after the King's architect.

Financial difficulties and the Revolution made it impossible for Louis XVI to pursue the work. However, from 1774 to 1777, he had the park replanted under the guidance of Hubert Robert who designed the Grove of the Baths of Apollo and replaced the Maze with the Queen's Grove.

On October 6, 1789, the Royal family was forced to leave the château for the Tuileries in Paris. The Revolution thus stripped Versailles of its vocation along with all of its furniture and works of art, and left an estate with unkempt gardens and buildings which served different purposes, some of which were of interest, such as the special museum of the École Française.

In 1806-1807, and in particular after his marriage to Marie-Louise of Austria in 1810, Napoleon wished to restore and refurnish the château after having completely refurbished the Grand and Petit Trianon. He started by commissioning the architect Dufour to build a pavilion to match the Gabriel Wing, which would only be completed under Louis XVIII. All of the tapestries that came to adorn the apartments were ordered from Lyon, and new furnishings were similarly introduced for certain apartments. From 1814 to 1824, Louis XVIII took over the projects and had all of the King's and Queen's apartments restored. His brother and successor, Charles X, did not pursue the restoration work and, when the 1830 Revolution arose, it was feared that Versailles would be abandoned and destroyed. However, Louis-

Philippe, a descendent of Monsieur, Louis XIV's brother, wished to save the château by transforming it into a "museum dedicated to the glories of France." From 1833 to 1837, the work was carried out and paid for

out of the Sovereign's private income, not without destroying some of the interior décor in order to arrange portraits and historical scenes in chronological or thematic order. The inauguration took place on June 10, 1837, during the celebrations held for the marriage of the Prince Royal.

A new life opened up for Versailles with some gradual reorientation resulting in a leaning towards contemporary descriptive and factual works, from the beginning of the 19th Century and, since the end of the Second World War, increasingly accurate restoration and refurnishing of the preserved apartments.

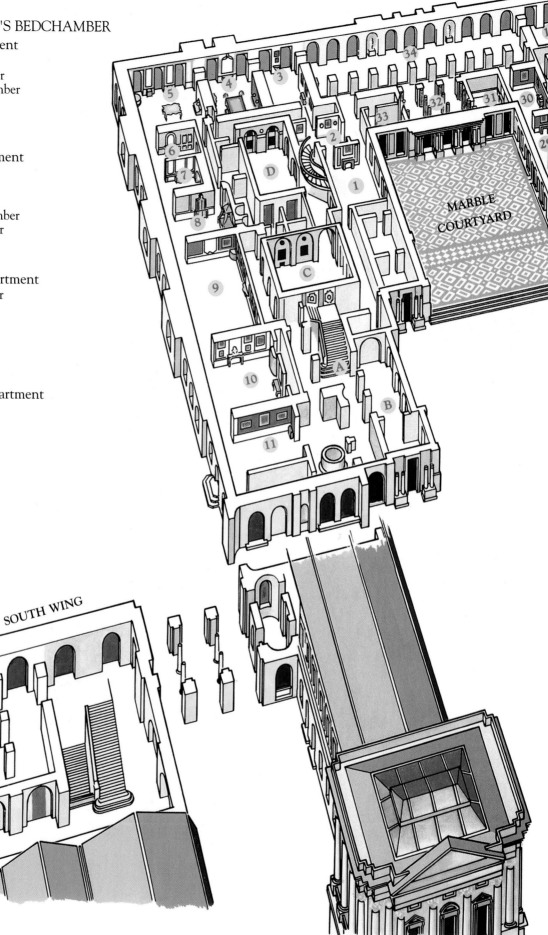

TOUR OF THE KING'S BEDCHAMBER

The Dauphin's Apartment
1 The Guardroom
2 The First Antechamber
3 The Second Antechamber
4 The Bedchamber
5 The State Cabinet
6 The Library

The Dauphine's Apartment
7 The Private Cabinet
8 The Bedchamber
9 The State Chamber
10 The Second Antechamber
11 The First Antechamber

THE OTHER TOURS

Madame Victoire's Apartment
12 The First Antechamber
13 The Salon des Nobles
14 The State Cabinet
15 The Bedchamber
16 The Private Cabinet
17 The Library

Madame Adélaïde's Apartment
18 The Private Cabinet
19 The Bedchamber
20 The State Cabinet

MARBLE COURTYARD

SOUTH WING

21 The Salle des Hocquetons (Archer's Room),
   formerly the drawing-room of the Ambassadors' Staircase
22 Vestibule to the former Ambassadors' Staircase
23 Vestibule
24 Room of the King's Guard
26 The King's Staircase

The Captain of the Guard's Apartment
27 The State Cabinet
28 The Private Cabinet
29 The Bedchamber

Marie-Antoinette's Apartment
30 (Room 30)
31 The Bedchamber
32 The Central Vestibule
33 The Bathroom

34 The Lower Gallery

A The Marble or Queen's Staircase
B The Vestibule to the Queen's Staircase
C The Monseigneur's or Queen's Courtyard
D The Dauphin's or Queen's Courtyard
E The King's Private Courtyard

NORTH WING

CHAPEL

TOUR OF THE STATE APARTMENTS

The State Apartment
1 The Drawing-Room of Plenty
2 The Venus Drawing-Room
3 The Diana Drawing-Room
4 The Mars Drawing-Room
5 The Mercury Drawing-Room
6 The Apollo Drawing-Room
7 The War Drawing-Room
8 The Peace Drawing-Room

The Queen's Apartment
9 The Queen's Bedchamber
10 The State Cabinet or Salon des Nobles
11 The Antechamber of the Grand Couvert
12 The Guardroom
13 The Marble (or Queen's) Staircase
14 The Loggia (also leading to
     the King's Apartment)

The Queen's Private Rooms
a The Bathroom
b The Annexe to the Library
c The Private Cabinet
d The Library
e The Meridian Cabinet
f The Duchesse de Bourgogne's Cabinet

Madame de Maintenon's Apartment
g-h Antechambers
i The Bedchamber
j The State Cabinet

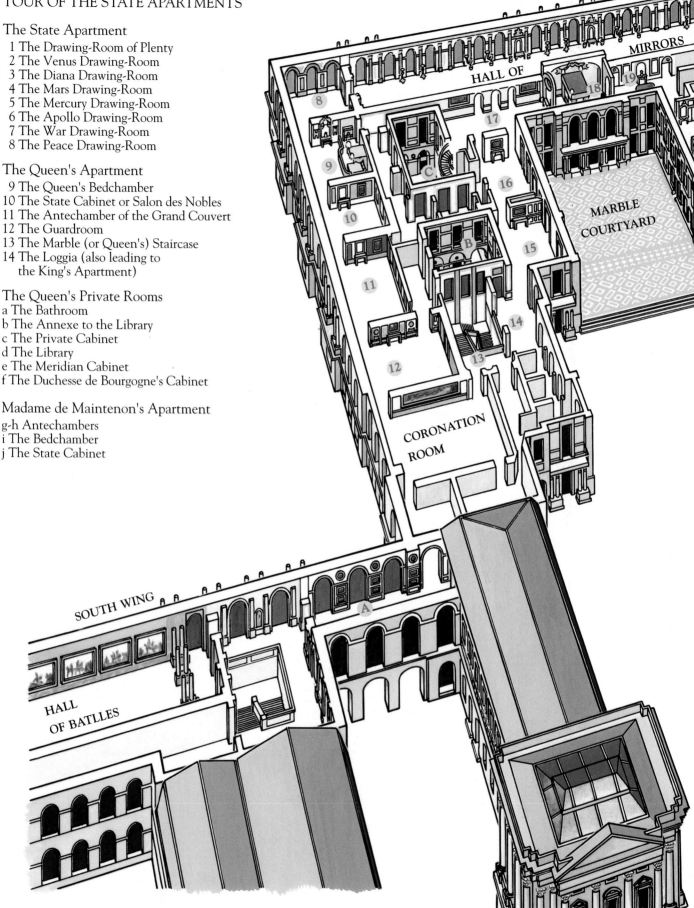

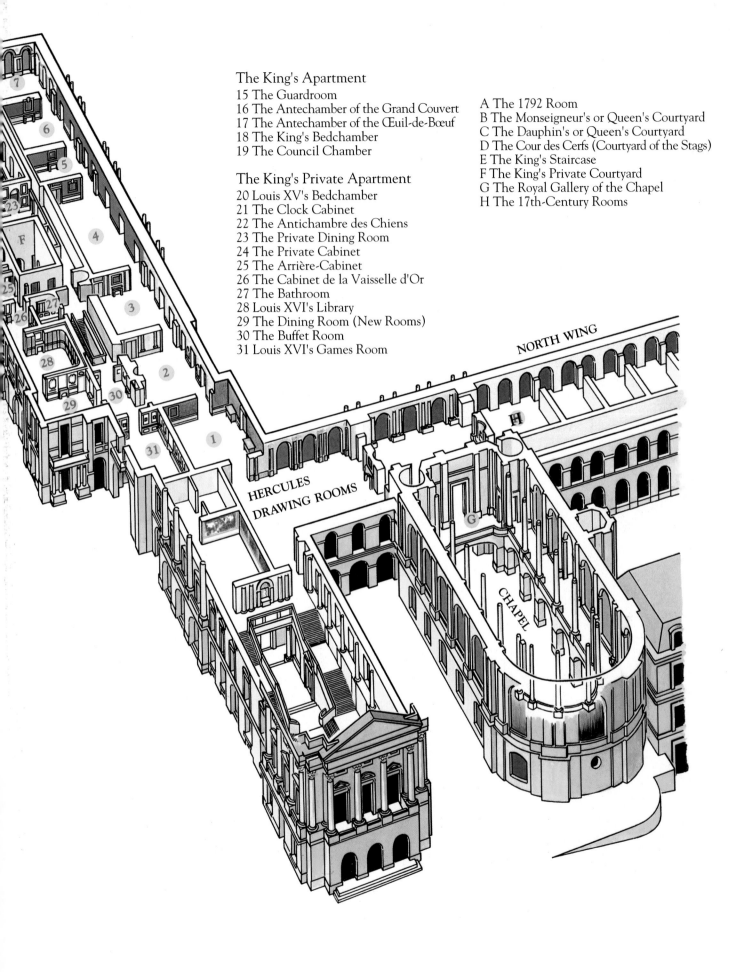

The King's Apartment

15 The Guardroom
16 The Antechamber of the Grand Couvert
17 The Antechamber of the Œuil-de-Bœuf
18 The King's Bedchamber
19 The Council Chamber

The King's Private Apartment

20 Louis XV's Bedchamber
21 The Clock Cabinet
22 The Antichambre des Chiens
23 The Private Dining Room
24 The Private Cabinet
25 The Arrière-Cabinet
26 The Cabinet de la Vaisselle d'Or
27 The Bathroom
28 Louis XVI's Library
29 The Dining Room (New Rooms)
30 The Buffet Room
31 Louis XVI's Games Room

A The 1792 Room
B The Monseigneur's or Queen's Courtyard
C The Dauphin's or Queen's Courtyard
D The Cour des Cerfs (Courtyard of the Stags)
E The King's Staircase
F The King's Private Courtyard
G The Royal Gallery of the Chapel
H The 17th-Century Rooms

NORTH WING

HERCULES
DRAWING ROOMS

CHAPEL

The Historical Galleries: the Crusades and Seventeenth-Century Galleries

Louis-Philippe, King of the French from 1830 to 1848, transformed Versailles into a museum dedicated to the glories of France. Through his desire to reconcile the different regimes, the Citizen King succeeded in creating the first museum of the history of France. He transformed the apartments of the princes and courtiers into vast galleries, in which the ancient paintings and sculptures were brought together in evocative retrospectives. The galleries devoted to the 17th Century are a good introduction to the tour of the royal apartments located on the first floor of the central body of the château.

The portraits of Le Nôtre and Colbert by Maratta and Lefevre, respectively, are highly representative of the figures who worked for Versailles. The latter, Controller General of Finances, Superintendent of the King's Buildings, was undoubtedly Louis XIV's best minister. Colbert died in 1689.

The large painting by Claude Hallé shown opposite, representing *The Audience given by Louis XIV to the Doge of Genoa in the Hall of Mirrors*, on May 15, 1685, allows us to have some idea of the silver furniture which adorned the rooms of the State Apartment.

The ceilings of the five Crusades Galleries are adorned with the coats of arms of the families who, in the Middle Ages, went to free the Holy Places. The most famous of the many paintings, all of which were retrospectives, was *The Entry of the Crusaders into Constantinople* by Delacroix (the original now in the Louvre has been replaced by a copy). This décor was to serve as a setting for the door of the Knights Hospital of the Holy Sepulchre in Rhodes, a gift to Louis-Philippe from the Ottoman Sultan.

The Royal Chapel

Following the tradition of the Palatine chapels, the Royal Chapel has two storeys. The galleries were reserved for the King, the royal family and important members of the Court, while the rest of the congregation occupied the ground floor. Consecrated in 1710, and dedicated to Saint Louis, ancestor and patron saint of the royal family, the chapel was the last building to be constructed at Versailles under the reign of Louis XIV.

The decoration of the ceiling depicts the continuity between *Old* and *New Testaments*, with its three constituent paintings referring to the Holy Trinity: in the centre, *The Glory of the Father Announcing the Coming of the Messiah*, by Antoine Coypel; above the altar, *The Resurrection of Christ*, by Charles de Lafosse; and above the Royal Gallery, *The Holy Spirit Descending upon the Virgin and the Apostles*, by Jean Jouvenet.

The Chapel Drawing-Room

To attend Mass the King had to cross this room, which links the Royal Gallery to the State Apartment. Its decoration is therefore related to that of the chapel, but the themes are more secular; two niches hold statues commissioned by Louis XV: *Glory holding the Medallion of Louis XV*, by Vassé, and *Royal Magnanimity*, by Bousseau.

The State Apartment

The State Apartment, thus named in contrast to the King's Private Apartments or Private Cabinets, was completed during the construction of the Hall of Mirrors and the War and Peace Drawing-Rooms from 1678 to 1686. After having been used as a dwelling for the King, the State Apartment was used both as a ceremonial apartment (some of the finest paintings from the royal collection are hung there) and as reception rooms during what was known as "apartment evenings": these took place on Monday, Wednesday and Thursday evenings from six until ten, and were the setting for the different diversions provided for the courtiers.

The Hercules Drawing-Room

This drawing-room was built as a setting for Veronese's *Meal at the House of Simon the Pharisee*, a gift to Louis XIV from the Republic of Venice in 1664. Built on the site of the fourth chapel used from 1682 to 1710, hence during the major part of the reign of Louis XIV at Versailles, the Hercules Drawing-Room, begun in 1712, was only finished in 1736 with the completion of François Lemoyne's ceiling representing *The Apotheosis of Hercules*.

The Drawing-Room of Plenty

This drawing-room originally gave onto the Cabinet of Curios and Rare Objects (today Louis XIV's Games Room), where were exhibited the most precious items from Louis XIV's collections. According to Mademoiselle de Scudéry, they were "vessels set with gold, with diamonds; others with agates encrusted with emeralds, turquoise, jade, pearls etc., Chinese and Japanese porcelain".

Thanks to the balustrade painted around the ceiling by Houasse, we have some idea of the objects in Louis XIV's rare objects collection. The most marvellous was the nef decorated with diamonds and rubies which held the King's napkin and cutlery, and which is depicted above the door, opposite the windows, surmounted by Royal Munificence.

The Venus Drawing-Room

On apartment evenings, the Venus Drawing-Room was used for the serving of light meals. The *Mercure Galant* reports that tables were set up there spread with silver dishes containing preserves and fresh and crystallised fruit. In addition to the perspectives painted in *trompe-l'œil* and the two statues of Meleager and Atalanta (also in *trompe-l'œil*), glorification of the sovereign here takes the form of a full-length statue by Jean Warin, representing Louis XIV as a Roman emperor. In the ceiling oval, René-Antoine Houasse painted the subject which gives this drawing-room its name, *The Goddess of Love subjugating the Gods and Powers*.

In 1752, the Ambassadors' Staircase, which until then had provided access to the State Apartment, and whose sumptuous décor had so impressed visitors, was destroyed. The Venus and Diana Drawing-Rooms still, however, retain the marble décor which matched that of the staircase, to which they served as upper vestibules.

The Diana Drawing-Room

Louis XIV, who was an excellent billiard-player, had a large
table set up here, covered when not in use with a crimson velvet cloth, its edges fringed with gold. The ladies followed the
game from benches set up on platforms, which gave them a good
view and allowed them to applaud the King's successes. The whole
of the decoration of this room refers to the legend of the goddess
Diana. Above the fireplace is Charles de Lafosse's *Sacrifice of Iphigenia*,
and opposite is *Diana Watching over the Sleeping Endymion* (1672) by Gabriel
Blanchard. The bust of Louis XIV opposite is the work of Bernini.

The Mars Drawing-Room

Until 1682, this drawing-room was used as a guardroom, which explains the war décor, in particular the cornice decorated alternately with helmets and trophies. It then changed its function, being used for concerts on apartment evenings, and between 1684 and 1750 there were galleries for musicians on either side of the chimney-breast.

Domenichino's *King David Playing the Harp* (opposite), mentioned in 1794 as being in the neighbouring Mercury Drawing-Room, has been placed where Veronese's *Mystic Marriage of Saint Catherine* hung during the reign of Louis XIV.

Mercury Drawing-Room

The Mercury and Apollo Drawing-Rooms were the most luxurious in the château of Versailles, in which was kept some of the famous silver furniture until it was melted in 1689. In 1682, when Court and Government were officially established at Versailles, the Mercury Drawing-Room was the State Bedchamber. For this original function, we have installed the bed commissioned by Louis-Philippe for the bedchamber of Louis XIV when Versailles was turned into a museum.

The central motif of the ceiling painted by Jean-Baptiste de Champaigne shows *Mercury in his Chariot Drawn by Two Cocks*. The same artist painted the ceiling-coves representing Alexander the Great and Ptolemy II surrounded by Scholars and Philosophers.

The automaton clock was a gift to Louis XIV from the clock-maker Antoine Morand in 1706. When the hour strikes, there appear the figures of Louis XIV and of Fame descending from a cloud. The clock, without doubt located here from only the 18th Century, gave the Mercury Drawing-Room the name of the Clock Drawing-Room.

The Apollo Drawing-Room

Versailles was the first royal château to have a throne room. The silver throne, measuring at least eight foot, was melted down in 1689, and was replaced much later, under Louis XV, by a gilt wood throne. The Apollo Drawing-Room was used for formal audiences. On the ceiling, Charles de Lafosse painted *The Chariot of the Sun* (see following page). The famous portrait of Louis XIV by Rigaud (opposite) hung in this room until the Revolution. The portrait of the reigning sovereign hung opposite, henceforth Louis XVI by Callet. A platform and the eye-bolts in the arch mouldings show where the throne and its dais once stood.

The War Drawing-Room

The War Drawing-Room evokes Louis XIV's victories over the allied powers during the war with Holland, and the Peace of Nijmegen which brought it to an end in 1678. The chimney-piece, designed by Le Brun, is decorated with bas-reliefs by Antoine Coysevox. The large medallion portrays an important episode of the war with Holland: Louis XIV is represented on horseback in classical dress on the occasion of the French troops' crossing of the Rhine on June 12, 1672. On the fireplace we can

see Clio, the Muse of History, writing the history of the King. In collaboration with Le Conte, Arcy and Prou, Coysevox executed the trophies which surmount the mirrored false doors, reflecting the same spirit as the bas-reliefs of the fireplace.

The Hall of Mirrors

The War Drawing-Room, the Hall of Mirrors and the Peace Drawing-Room form an ensemble whose décor is devoted to the military victories and political successes of Louis XIV. This ensemble is not contemporary with the first major works carried out by the architect Le Vau. In the plan for a stone envelope around Louis XIII's little château, which he presented in 1668, the latter left a terrace on the west façade overlooking the gardens. It was Jules Hardouin-Mansart who on September 26, 1678 (the year of the Peace of Nijmegen) presented the King with plans for the construction of the present Hall of Mirrors. Work began immediately, and was completed in 1686. Under the Ancien Régime, the Hall of Mirrors functioned as a passageway giving access to the King's Apartment. Here gathered the courtiers who hoped to see the monarch when each morning he made his way to the Chapel. Some took the opportunity to present some request. When he received extraordinary embassies, such as that of Siam in 1686, Louis XIV would have the silver throne moved here from its usual place in the Apollo Drawing-Room. Grand celebrations were also held here, such as full-dress balls, or the masked balls given on the occasion of princely marriages.

At first, Louis XIV had the Hall of Mirrors furnished with pieces in solid silver designed by Charles Le Brun. However, these were melted down in 1689 to meet the expenses of war. These original fittings were candelabra, pedestal tables, and tables for torches, and great vases to hold orange-trees, all finely worked by the finest silversmiths of the time.

The Hall of Mirrors

In his ceiling-painting, Charles Le Brun portrayed the history of Louis XIV's reign, and its central theme is the war against Holland and its allies (1672-1678) and the War of Devolution (1667-1668).

The whole composition is organised around a central motif entitled *The King Governs Alone*, in which one sees Louis XIV, face to face with the great European powers, turn away from his games and pleasures to contemplate the crown of immortality held out to him by Glory, and which is pointed out to him by Mars, the god of war.

The candelabra were replaced in 1770 on the occasion of the marriage of the then future Louis XVI with the Archiduchesse Marie-Antoinette de Lorraine-Autriche. These are the candelabra which were reconstructed by moulding the six original preserved models, kept in the Apollo Drawing-Room. This is the same for the twenty-four chandeliers which used to be hung only during evening celebrations.

The Peace Drawing-Room

As its name suggests, the decoration of this drawing-room is dedicated to peace: the peace which followed the wars represented in the War Drawing-Room and the Hall of Mirrors, and that established by the Kings of France as an expression of France's dominant place in Europe.

Above the fireplace is a painting by François Lemoine (1729), showing *Louis XV offering Europe an olive-branch*. This drawing-room was soon connected to the Queen's Apartment, to be used as the Games Room. It was thus separated from the Hall of Mirrors by a moving partition which closed off the connecting archway. Here, every Sunday, under the reign of Louis XV, the Queen Maria Leczinska gave concerts of sacred and secular music which played an important role in the musical life of Versailles.

The Queen's Apartment

The characteristic symmetry which marks Versailles existed from the beginning between the Queen's Apartment and the King's. Both had the same number of rooms, the decoration of the ceilings was devoted to the same deities and planets, and they differed only in the paintings of the ceiling-coves, which in the King's Apartment portrayed male, and in the Queen's, female figures.

The Queen's Bedchamber

It was in this room, in public, that the Queen gave birth to the heirs to the throne. In her *Memoirs*, Madame Campan, who was Marie-Antoinette's First Woman of the Bedchamber, described what such a birth could be like: "the moment that Vermond the accoucheur announced 'The Queen is about to give birth', the crowds of spectators who rushed into her room were so numerous and disorderly that one thought the Queen would perish... Two Savoyards got up on the furniture the more easily to see the Queen, who was facing the fireplace on a bed got ready for her labour."

The Salon des Nobles

In the Salon des Nobles, the Queen of France held official audiences, and ladies newly admitted to Court were presented to her. Certain elements of the décor, the ceiling in particular, which portrays an allegory of Mercury, recall the fact that originally the Queen's Apartment was symmetrical with the King's. The furniture is that designed for Marie-Antoinette in 1785.

The Antechamber of the Grand Couvert

In Queen Maria-Theresa's day, this room was the Room of the Queen's Guard, hence the ceiling decorated with warlike themes. Visitors who had obtained an audience with the Queen would have to wait here before entering the Salon des Nobles or the Bedchamber. This room was also used for concerts and theatrical performances. The name Grand Couvert comes from that of the ceremonial requiring that the King and Queen eat certain meals in public. One of the most noteworthy was the meal that Louis XV and Maria Leczinska took here in the company of the young Mozart on January 1, 1764.

Out of the paintings hung in the Antechamber of the Grand Couvert, the most famous is the large painting by Madame Vigée-Lebrun exhibited in the 1787 Drawing-Room. The painting depicts Marie-Antoinette with her three children: Madame Royale who survived the Revolution; the Duke of Normandy, future Louis XVII, who died in the Prison du Temple in 1795; and the Dauphin, who died in 1789, pointing to an empty cradle which should have held Madame Sophie, who died at a very young age before the painting was completed.

The Guardroom

This room, set aside for the use of the Queen's guards, was constantly cluttered with screens hiding camp-beds, tables and racks for their arms. It was here that on the morning of October 6, 1789, guards lost their lives helping the Queen seek refuge by the King's side.

In the corners of the ceiling, Noël Coypel painted the figures of courtiers leaning over into the room, watching the comings and goings.

The Historical Galleries: the Salle du Sacre

This room was originally the site of the château's third chapel. When in 1682 the Court and Government were officially established at Versailles, it served as the common guardroom of the King's and Queen's guards. Permanently cluttered with the sedan chairs of the ladies of the court, benches, screens and arms racks, and hung with painted canvas, courtiers nicknamed this room the "magasin" or storeroom. Here every Maundy Thursday, the King would wash the feet of thirteen poor children. Its present appearance and name date from the reign of Louis-Philippe who installed the painting by David, depicting the coronation of Napoleon I on December 2, 1804.

The Historical Galleries: the Hall of Battles

Situated in the South Wing (or Princes' Wing), covering the first floor and the attic on the park side, the Hall of Battles took the place of the apartments reserved for the members of the royal family. The architects Nepveu and Fontaine designed the Hall of Battles as a setting for the vast paintings dedicated to the great French victories, from Tolbiac, won by Clovis in 497, to Wagram, a victory for Napoleon in 1809. It was Louis-Philippe's express desire for the busts of the great officers and princes of royal blood who died for France to be exhibited in the Hall of Battles, along with the commemorative plaques bearing their names and dates. A complement to the Hall of Mirrors, it leads to the 1830 room, created to honour Louis-Philippe's accession to the throne and the new constitutional monarchy born out of the 1830 Revolution.

The paintings forming the décor of the Hall of Battles are not of equal quality: *Marignan* by Evariste Fragonard, *The Entry of Henry IV into Paris* and *The Battle of Austerlitz* by Gérard are striking. However, Delacroix's *Saint Louis in Taillebourg* (detail above) is particularly famous for the artist's skill in creating an ardent and romantic image of an event that took place over six hundred years previously.

TOUR OF THE KING'S BEDCHAMBER

The King's Apartment

The King's Apartment consists of a guardroom, two ante-chambers, a bedchamber and a large cabinet, generally referred to as the Council Chamber. It is reached via the Marble Staircase, also called the Queen's Staircase because it originally served only Queen Maria-Theresa's Apartment. In 1681 it replaced a more modest staircase and, after the death of the Queen in 1683, was used to reach Louis XIV's new apartment. It was designed as a worthy match for the Ambassadors' Staircase.

The Marble Staircase

In addition to the marble décor and the gilt lead sculpture by Massou symbolising the marriage of Louis XIV and Maria-Theresa, the Marble Staircase is adorned with a vast painting showing a palace perspective, the architecture of which was painted by Meusnier, the people by Poerson and the flowers by Belin de Fontenay.

The Guardroom and the Antechamber of the Grand Couvert

The Guardroom is decorated exclusively with white panelling; above the fireplace is Parrocel's painting of the *Battle of Leuze*, a tribute to the King's guards who distinguished themselves in 1691 under the orders of the Maréchal de Luxembourg. More richly decorated than the Guardroom, the First Antechamber was used every evening, under Louis XIV, for the Grand Couvert, that is, the meal that the King took in public. The King's table stood before the fireplace, his spoon, his knife and his fork were brought in a box wrought of gold called the Cadenas, hence the expression "*mettre le couvert*" or "to lay the table". The food was paraded with great pomp from the Grand Commun. Every Monday morning in the First Antechamber, a table was set out covered with a green velvet cloth, behind which the King was symbolically represented by an empty armchair: here courtiers could table their petitions, which were never left unanswered.

The Antechamber of the Œil-de-Bœuf

The Second Antechamber, known as the *Œil-de-Bœuf* due to shape of the window in the cornice of the room, was only enlarged to its present size in 1701. It served as a "waiting room" for the ceremonies of the *Lever* and the *Coucher*, when the King rose or retired. The paintings by Bassan were replaced by different portraits of the royal family during the reign of Louis XIV, with, in particular, a large mythological composition by Jean Nocret (opposite).

The King's Bedchamber

This central room was originally the State Drawing-Room. After the death of Queen Maria-Theresa, it was attached to the King's apartment and became generally known as "the room in which the King dresses". At that time, three archways opened onto the Hall of Mirrors for which the room acted as a sort of complement. In 1701, Louis XIV decided to turn the room into his bedchamber; the above painting by François Marot shows it as it was at the time. It was here that the Sun King would die on September 1, 1715. After him, both Louis XV and Louis XVI would continue to use it for the ceremonies of the *Lever* and the *Coucher*. It was on the balcony, October 6, 1789, that Louis XVI, the Queen and the Dauphin appeared before the crowd as the royal family was forced to leave Versailles for Paris.

The King's Bedchamber

In 1701, when the State Drawing-Room became the bedchamber, the archways opening onto the Hall of Mirrors were closed off and replaced by an alcove hung with velvet in the winter to match the furnishings, and brocade in the summer (embroidered with gold thread). It is the summer furnishings that were restored. At the same time, Coustou carved the relief depicting *France watching over the sleeping King*, which dominates the King's bed.

Among the paintings embedded in the panelling and which still remain in place, two in particular typify the interests of Louis XIV: self-portrait by Van Dyck and *Caesar's Denarius* by Valentin de Boulogne.

The Council Chamber

The former State Cabinet of Louis XIV and the King's Wig Cabinet were joined together in 1755 to form the present Council Chamber where one can observe in the panelling carved by Rousseau to designs by Gabriel medallions evoking the work of the King. The Council of State met here on Sundays and Wednesdays, and occasionally on Mondays, while the Council of Finances met on Tuesdays and Saturdays. Once or twice a month there would be Extraordinary Councils, such as the Council of Despatches. The King would be seated in an armchair and the ministers on folding chairs. Also, during the reign of Louis XIV and his successors, the King would summon his family here for certain ceremonies, such as the signing of the registers during princely marriages. It was also here that, in 1700, Louis XIV accepted the Spanish crown for his grandson the Duc d'Anjou from whom Juan Carlos, the current King of Spain, descends.

The Dauphin's and Dauphine's Apartments

A small staircase, its present appearance dating from the reign of Louis XVI, leads down to the Antechamber of the Oeil-de-Boeuf in the Dauphin's Apartment, the library of which communicates with the Dauphine's Apartment. They aim to depict the surroundings in which the Dauphin, son of Louis XV, father of Louis XVI, lived with his wife Maria-Josepha of Saxony. Despite the changes made by Louis-Philippe, some of the rooms retain all or part of their panelling, namely the Dauphin's bedchamber (below), his State Cabinet and Library (opposite), together with the Dauphine's Private Cabinet (right page). It should not be forgotten that, during the 17th Century, the Grand Dauphin, son of Louis XIV, turned it into an apartment renowned for its beauty and lavish collections, which, during the infancy of Louis XV, was to become the abode of the Regent Philippe d'Orléans.

Although it has not been possible to retrieve all of the furnishings which adorned these apartments, at least certain objects were found: the globe commissioned in 1781 by Louis XIV from the geographer Mancelle, for the education of his son; the desk by Bernard Van Rysenburgh and Oeben, delivered for the Dauphin in 1756, and constantly used by Louis XVI in his library under the eaves, in then his Privy Purse Cabinet; or the bureau delivered in 1745 by B.V.R.B. for the first Dauphine and reused by the Dauphine of Saxony; and the commode by Gaudreaux, delivered for the Dauphine's bedchamber at Fontainebleau.

The King's Private Apartment

Named the King's Private Apartment during the reign of Louis XIV, this suite was known as the Interior Apartment under Louis XV and Louis XVI. After having been reserved solely for the Sovereign's collections during the reign of the Great King, it became a proper apartment in 1737, where Louis XV then Louis XVI actually lived.

Louis XV's Bedchamber

When, in 1738, Louis XV decided to install a bedchamber smaller than that of Louis XIV, he still continued to use his grandfather's bedchamber for the ceremonies of the *Lever* and the *Coucher*. It was in here that he died of smallpox on May 10, 1774. It was also here that Louis XVI spent his last night at Versailles, from the 5th to the 6th of October 1789.

The Clock Cabinet

Constituting two rooms, the second of which led through an archway into the next, and forming the cabinets in which Louis XIV exhibited some of his paintings, the Clock Cabinet underwent several transformations under Louis XV before acquiring its definitive appearance in 1760, in order to set off the astronomical clock designed by Passamant, kept in this room from 1754. Delamaire's barometer, commissioned by Louis XV, delivered during the reign of Louis XVI and only installed under Charles X in 1827, stands opposite.

The complex mechanism of the astronomical clock enables it to tell the time, the day of the week, the date in the month, the month, the year and the phase of the moon. Inside the crystal globe above one can see the planets revolving around the sun according to Copernican principles.

The Private Cabinet

Having been transformed several times, the Work Cabinet or Private Cabinet acquired its definitive décor in 1760. The magnificent panelling both here and in the Clock Cabinet had been previously carved by Verbeckt and still remains today. The large roll-top desk commissioned from Oeben and Riesener dates from the reign of Louis XV (1759-1769).

Louis XVI's Library

Like the previous room, known as the Cabinet de la Vaisselle d'Or, and the following, known as the Porcelain Dining Room, the Library is on the site of the old Ambassadors' Staircase and the Petite Galerie. It was created on Louis XVI's accession to the throne, in 1774. Of its original furniture, in addition to the globes representing the earth and the planets, the table still remains, the top being made from a single piece measuring 2.10 metres in diameter.

The Porcelain Dining Room

This room reached its present size in 1769 when Louis XV joined his daughter Madame Adélaïde's Apartment to his private cabinets. However, the furniture and fabric are those designed in 1785 for Louis XVI. The different porcelain pieces all originate from royal services. They serve as a reminder that every year, towards Christmas, the King would exhibit in this room the latest Sèvres porcelain. Everyone could admire and buy them.

The walls are hung with Sèvres porcelain plaques painted after Oudry's tapestries depicting the royal hunts of Louis XV and transposed here to represent the hunts of Louis XVI in the forests of Compiègne and Fontainebleau. These plaques were already part of the décor under the Ancien Régime.

Louis XVI's Games Room

During the reign of Louis XIV, this was the Cabinet of Curios and Rare Objects, where were exhibited some of the most precious items from the royal collections. Madame Adélaïde's antechamber in 1753, the Cabinet of Curios and Rare Objects was completely transformed in 1769 for Louis XV who wanted to turn it into a library, plans which Louis XVI moved elsewhere to install his Games Room here instead. It was for this purpose that the chairs designed by Boulard were commissioned in 1785, and have now returned to their proper place. The corner cupboards delivered by Riesener in 1775 and the paintings by Van Blarenberghe also originated in this room. The latter were gouaches commissioned by Louis XVI to commemorate the different victories of his grandfather Louis XV.

The King's Private Cabinets

The King's Private Cabinets is the name given to a suite of rooms above the King's Private Apartment, which was the private domain of Louis XV and Louis XVI. The library and its annexes, and the Geography and Physics Cabinets illustrate the kings' interest in scholarship and research. Some rooms also became apartments for the King's intimates.

The King's Staircase

This staircase led to both the King's Private Apartment and Private Cabinets. It was the scene of the attempt on the life of Louis XV on January 5, 1757, by Damiens, as the King was getting ready to leave for Trianon.

Madame du Barry's Library

Created in 1753 for Madame Adélaïde when the princess lived in the present new rooms, it acquired its definitive appearance in 1769, when it was joined to Madame Barry's Apartment which occupied part of the King's Private Cabinets.

Marie-Antoinette's Private Rooms

Now reduced to just a few rooms (oratory, bathroom), the Queen's Private Cabinets were at their largest in the time of Marie-Antoinette. The Queen had use of not only Maria Leczinska's private cabinets on the first floor, but also a suite of small rooms located on the second floor, around the inner courtyards, and a proper apartment on the ground floor where Madame Sophie, Aunt of Louis XVI, had lived until her death in 1782.

The Queen's Private Cabinet

This replaced the night apartment of the Duc de Bourgogne, father of Louis XV, and Maria Leczinska's private cabinet, and was granted to Marie-Antoinette who received her favourite artists, the painter, Madame Vigée-Lebrun, the composer Gluck, her old music-teacher, and Mlle Bertin, her dress-maker.

The Meridian Cabinet

After having once been Maria Leczinska's private drawing-room, a staircase was built here in 1770, connecting the Dauphin's Apartment, the future Louis XVI, to that of his wife Marie-Antoinette, who already occupied the Queen's Apartment. The present drawing-room was fitted out in 1781 on the birth of the first Dauphin. The décor of the panelling serves as a reminder of the event, as do the carvings on the console.

In her *Memoirs*, Madame Campan, Marie-Antoinette's First Woman of the Bedchamber, states that "The list of people received in the Queen's private rooms had been given to the Ushers of the Bedchamber by the Princess de Lamballe, and the people listed there could avail themselves of this favour only on days when the Queen desired the company of her intimates... Persons of the first rank at Court would sometimes ask her for private audiences."

The Mesdames' Apartments

The only remaining apartments belonging to the daughters of Louis XV are those occupied by Madame Adélaïde and Madame Victoire from 1769 until the Revolution. These apartments replaced Louis XIV's former Bath Apartment, altered to make apartments for Madame de Pompadour and the Comtesse de Toulouse. According to Madame Campan, "Louis XV went down to Madame Adélaïde's apartment each morning by a hidden staircase. He often brought and drank coffee that he had made himself. Madame Adélaïde would tug at a bell-pull, which would warn Madame Victoire of the King's visit…"

The Royal Opera

Louis XIV commissioned the first plans for the Royal Opera from Mansart and Vigarani in 1682; however, wars and financial difficulties towards the end of his reign meant that it could not be built. The second design, for the same location at the end of the North Wing, was presented by Gabriel to Louis XV in 1748, but still failed to be built. It was only after the marriage of the Dauphin, the future Louis XVI, to the Archiduchesse Marie-Antoinette, that the work was carried out and the opera finally completed and inaugurated on May 16, 1770.

The opera-house is in the shape of a truncated ellipse. It was entirely built of wood for reasons of economy and rapidity, which provides excellent acoustics. Its imitation marble décor is embellished with sculptures by Pajou, and the ceiling painted by Durameau represents the triumph of Apollo, god of the arts. The architect Gabriel and the engineer Arnoult had planned a mechanism which would raise the floor of the auditorium to the same level as the stage, decorated to match the rest of the room. The theatre would then be able to host full-dress balls, dances where the ladies wore jewellery, tiaras and formal dress.

The Consulate, Empire and Restoration-to-1914 Rooms

In his desire to reconcile the different regimes, Louis-Philippe decided not to favour a particular period of French history. He thus devoted the whole of the ground floor of the South Wing to the Empire, to which should be added the second-floor rooms, above the Queen's Apartment and the South Wing, running alongside the vault of the Hall of Battles.

Among the works devoted to this short but turbulent period of French history, stretching from the Revolution to the end of the Empire, the portrait of General Bonaparte at the Pont d'Arcole on November 17, 1796, by Gros, is surely one of the most magnificent.

Portrait of Louis XVIII by Gérard

When he regained the throne of his ancestors in 1814, Louis XVIII wanted to be painted in the full pomp of the monarchy. The painter Gérard depicted the Sovereign in royal dress, even though, unlike his brother Charles X, his coronation could not take place at Reims due to the strains of the ceremony on his health. These are, however, the royal robes (now kept in Saint-Denis) which were to decorate his hearse (kept in the Coach Museum) during his funeral in 1824.

Louis-Philippe and his Sons in front of the Château of Versailles, by Horace Vernet

Proud of having saved Versailles, Louis-Philippe wanted to be painted in front of the open gate of the château accompanied by his sons. Having succeeded in turning Versailles into a memorial, he was keen to oversee the work that he paid for out of his own private income.

WALKS IN THE GARDENS

To the West

Beyond the château, to the west, stretch the gardens and the park, laid out around a main east-west axis, perpendicular to the château, and a secondary axis from north to south, running alongside the façades.

The Water Parterre

At the foot of the buildings, Le Nôtre created the parterres, designed to be viewed from the terraces. They were also intended to set off the château's architecture. The two perfectly horizontal ponds of the Water Parterre, mirrors reflecting the façades, which were dug considerably later (towards 1685), demonstrate this concept pushed to the extreme.

Statues of stone, marble, lead and bronze populate the gardens with people and animals, often derived from mythology or allegories. Le Nôtre made sure that the sculptures emphasised rather than interfered with the lines of the garden. Thus, several powerful recumbent figures came to adorn the edges of the Water Parterre. These bronze masterpieces depict the rivers of France, symbols of the kingdom.

The Grand Perspective

Openness and scope characterise the work of Le Nôtre. Before him, the gardens were closed and relatively modest in size. They now open onto the surrounding countryside and have changed scale. Le Nôtre also gives greater importance to the central axis, around which all of the other parts of the garden have been arranged. Starting from the terrace of the château, the Grand Perspective draws the eye to the horizon. As it moves further away, it crosses the parterres, descends through the groves, follows the canal between the forests of the park, gently rising through the countryside towards the sky. Thus making its way from a strongly architectural to a more natural setting, the axial route starts with a simple pathway between the ponds of the Water Parterre, goes down the steps, and skirts round the Fountain of Latona. After a small slope and another pathway between the Latona Parterres, it passes through the long grassy stretch of the Royal Avenue or Tapis Vert, bordered on either side with greenery, and opens onto the Fountain of Apollo and its vast esplanade, before merging with the Grand Canal 1650 metres in length.

The Fountain of Latona tells the story taken from Ovid's *Metamorphoses*, an ancient masterpiece providing numerous themes for the décor of Versailles. An episode from Apollo's childhood is depicted here. His mother Latona, having been ridiculed by the Lycian peasants, beseeches Jupiter for vengeance, who then turns them into frogs.

The Fountain of Apollo

This vast pond owes its décor, which deals with the major theme of the mythological, symbolical and political concepts developed throughout the gardens, to its prime position. Just as Louis XIV is identified with the sun god, Phoebus Apollo, similarly, Apollo rising above the waves denotes the rising of the sun and the dawning of a promising reign. Le Brun, who designed the sculptures, expanded on the theme: he shows the god in his chariot drawn by four horses, surrounded by four Tritons and four sea monsters. He entrusted the execution of the sculpture to one of the most talented sculptors, Jean-Baptiste Tubi, a Roman in the King's service.

Like all of the exceptional royal commissions, the Apollo sculpture was executed at the Gobelins works. Cast between 1668 and 1670, it was gilded after its installation.

To the North

A natural slope leads from the Water Parterre to the Fountain of Neptune.

The décor of the fountains of the North Parterre matches the sculptures of marine deities adorning the façades of the North Wing. It also serves as a reminder of the closeness of two elements that have now disappeared: Louis XIV's Bath Apartment and the Grotto of Thetis. Tritons, Sirens, dolphins and crayfish populate the Pyramid Fountain and the two Crown ponds.

The North Parterre

Planted out with box trees and grass, brightened up with a few flowers and dotted with trimmed yew trees (topiaries), the North Parterre embraces the incline of the North Wing.

At the threshold of the Water Avenue, a long bas-relief (by F. Girardon, like the Pyramid) reveals the Bathing Nymphs through a curtain of water (which Louis XIV called "the sheet").

The Dragon Fountain and the Fountain of Neptune

Dominated by two large open-air pools, the Water Avenue, leading to the Dragon Fountain, separates two groves currently undergoing restoration. It is also called the Allée des Marmousets since it is lined with twenty-two bronze sculptures of children (after Le Brun's designs). These figures alternate with topiaries grown in the unusual shapes in which Louis XIV's gardeners used to trim the yew trees. Below the Dragon Fountain, the immense Fountain of Neptune comprises 58 jets and 147 hydraulic effects. Depending on the shape of the pipe outlets, the water shoots out in bubbles, waves, streams or showers. Beyond the fountain, a densely wooded area closes off the park, protecting it from the north wind.

In the Dragon Fountain (one of the oldest in Versailles), the water theme merges with the legend of Apollo, since the dragon in actual fact symbolises Python, the mythical serpent that Apollo slew with his bow and arrow. The water jet shooting out of the dragon's mouth, reaching up to 27 metres, is the highest of all of the fountains.

Built by Le Nôtre, the Fountain of Neptune was originally decorated with only the large lead vases around its edge. Sixty years later, continuing the work of his great grandfather, Louis XV enhanced it with monumental statues, also made of lead, symbolising Neptune and Amphitrite, Oceanus and Proteus.

To the South

Instead of natural slopes on this side, there is a series of three terraces: on the same level as the château is the South Parterre, the end of which drops vertically onto the Orangery; further along and lower down is the Pond of the Swiss, the exaggerated length of which was calculated to enhance the perspective.

The South Parterre

Its arrangement of box trees interspersed with flowers is landscaped in arabesques beneath the windows of the Queen's Apartment.

Through its vast space (main gallery 155 metres long and 13 metres high), simple lines and beautiful arches, the Orangery is one of the places in which Jules Hardouin-Mansart most successfully displayed his talents as a great architect.

The Orangery

The Orangery is tucked away underground below the château. Flanked with the great 100-step stairway, it ensures the stability of the grounds. Its south-facing position and double-glazing stabilise the temperature at between 5 and 8°C in winter. It houses 1080 delicate trees, all of which are planted in boxes: orange trees from Portugal and Italy, lemon trees and pomegranate trees (some of which are over 200 years old), oleanders, and palm trees (since the turn of the century). The trees produce little fruit since they are pruned into a decorative spherical form. The gardeners bring them out in mid-May and take them back inside in mid-October.

In the distance, the vast expanse of the Pond of the Swiss, the name of which refers to the contribution of the reinforcement regiments called in to drain the marshes and dig the pond. This was at the time when there were over 15,000 men working at Versailles.

The Avenues and Groves

Away from the central avenue, the surrounding wooded areas are waiting to be discovered, criss-crossed with a regular network of avenues. The wider, longer avenues, providing distant views, intersect at right angles. Other pathways, curved and diagonal, shorter and more narrow, lead to the groves (eight in the north and six in the south). From the large avenues, only walls of foliage can be seen. In the reign of Louis XIV, these walls of trees were espaliered at a great height and the foliage of the trees fixed to the frames was not allowed to grow over 15 metres. The strictly cubic appearance of these wooded areas reflected the desire of the King and his gardener to create a veritable architectural structure of foliage. In contrast to the rigid appearance of the outside, fantasy reigned within, surprising visitors with varied water effects in the midst of clearings in which the rockwork, trellis-work or architectural décor was enhanced by numerous sculptures. From the 17th Century, a number of regulations intervened concerning access to the groves, sometimes accessible to all, sometimes strictly limited. They can now be seen through their railings, or better still, entered during guided tours or during the Grandes-Eaux, when the fountains play at Versailles.

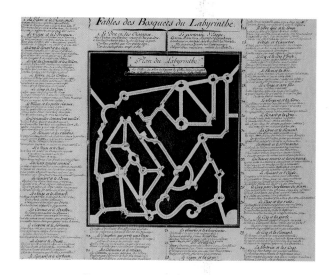

Since their creation, some of the groves have been subjected to alterations. Among these, the renowned Maze Grove (a map of which is shown above) was decorated with 39 fountains illustrating the Fables of La Fontaine, and then sadly replaced by the Queen's Grove in the time of Marie-Antoinette.

The Fountains of the Seasons

The Fountain of Bacchus decorates one of the four ponds placed at the intersection in the Avenues of the Four Seasons: Bacchus or Autumn, Saturn or Winter, Flora or Spring, Ceres or Summer. They served as a reminder that the sun god determined not only the course of the day, but also the course of the year.

Two major avenues, running parallel to the Grand Perspective, cut through the walls of foliage concealing the groves. These are bordered with lines of trees, rigorously pruned both in height and thickness, forming smaller avenues on either side. These are the Avenues of the Four Seasons.

The Ballroom and the Colonnade

The Ballroom (or Bosquet des Rocailles) and the Colonnade have been preserved as they were in the reign of Louis XIV. Almost contemporary with each other (both were created between 1680 and 1690), they are, nonetheless, very different since one was designed by a gardener, André Le Nôtre, and the other, by an architect, Jules Hardouin-Mansart. One makes use of natural elements: streams of water, rockwork and shells, vegetation covering the embankments and terraces. The other, a cold, formal peristyle of 32 columns surrounding Girardon's masterpiece, *The Rape of Persephone* by Pluto, is purely architecture and sculpture, marble and water. When Louis XIV asked Le Nôtre his opinion on the Colonnade, the gardener replied, "Sire, you turned a stonemason into a gardener, he has played you one of his tricks".

Louis XIV thought so highly of his gardens that he wrote "The Manner of Presenting the Gardens of Versailles" and had them painted by several artists. This gouache by Cotelle shows that the centre of the Ballroom was originally occupied by an island reached by small bridges. The Court could there be entertained by dinners, light refreshments, ballets or musical interludes, as in the other groves.

The Bosquet des Dômes and Enceladus

These two groves, adjacent to the fountain of Apollo, illustrate two trends in French art at the time of Louis XIV. The serenity of the Bosquet des Dômes contrasts with the cruel, dramatic effect of the Fountain of Enceladus.

The Bosquet des Dômes

Enceladus, leader of the giants, rebelled against Jupiter. In order to attack Mount Olympus, he piled mountain upon mountain. However, struck down by Jupiter, he disappeared, crushed under the rocks, uttering a final curse symbolised by the powerful jet shooting out of his mouth. [Gaspard Marsy (1675-1677) based on a design by Le Brun].

The Fountain of Enceladus had considerably deteriorated since the 17th Century. It has recently been fully restored to how it was in approximately 1700, a time when, having reached maturity, the gardens of Versailles were in a state of perfection. The trelliswork supporting sweet-scented plants were renewed, along with the small rockwork fountains, the entire hydraulic system and the triple turf-covered treads. The statue of the giant was also fully restored.

The Baths of Apollo

The Grove of the Baths of Apollo, concealed by the surrounding greenery, is particularly striking due to its size and broken relief. It was created almost a century after the older groves. It was during the replanting of the park ordered by Louis XVI in 1775 that the painter Hubert Robert completely redesigned the existing grove in which the three remarkable sculptures were already found: Apollo Served by Nymphs, and the two lateral groups, The Horses of the Sun, Groomed by the Tritons. Louis XIV had originally commissioned these works for the Grotto of Thetis. This grotto, sheltered beneath a pool, was a cool, precious place, with a carpet of shells and mirrors, the marine dwelling of the nymph, and night-time refuge of Phoebus Apollo. It had to be destroyed during the construction of the North Wing. Hubert Robert takes up the idea of the grotto again, but treats it according to the 18th-Century liking for wild nature with rocks and waterfalls.

This group is the sculptural masterpiece of Versailles. It depicts the morning ablutions of the deity as he prepares for his daily course, after having rested at the nymph Thetis' abode. Composed of seven figures carved in white marble, it was executed by François Girardon, who carved the four main figures, and Thomas Regnaudin, who carved the three nymphs in the background. Girardon was Louis XIV's favourite sculptor. A great friend and close colleague of Le Brun and Le Nôtre, he appears in all the major sites. His masters were Classical Antiquity and Nature. Here, this fluid, majestic young god recaptures the features of the famous Apollo Belvedere. The delicate flesh tones, the flowing robes, and the precision of the engravings on the plates bear witness to the sensitivity and brilliance of the artist.

THE CHATEAUX DE TRIANON

The Grand Trianon

In 1668, Louis XIV bought a village named Trianon, which he joined to the Versailles estate and demolished. A pavilion decorated with blue and white tiles, which became known as the Porcelain Trianon, was built there in 1670. In 1687, the King decided to replace it with a larger building, the work of Mansart, which became known as the Marble Trianon from the way in which it was decorated. From then on until the fall of the Second Empire in 1870, the Trianon was constantly inhabited, apart from during the Revolution. However, it is mainly the installations commissioned by Napoleon I and Louis-Philippe that still remain in this dwelling, fully restored in 1965 by order of General de Gaulle.

The Emperor's Bedchamber
Louis XV's Former State Cabinet, this room successively became the bedchamber of Napoleon, Princess Louise, then Princess Clothilde, Louis-Philippe's daughters. Louis-Philippe often visited Trianon while work was being carried out to convert Versailles into a museum. The room has been restored to how it was in the time of Napoleon, with his fawn, purple and silver silks.

The Mirror Drawing-Room
Strikingly decorated with mirrors, hence its name, this vast room in turn served as a state cabinet for the princes who inhabited the Left Wing of Trianon, Louis XIV himself, then his son the Grand Dauphin. After the Revolution, Madame, mother of Emperor Napoleon, Empress Marie-Louise and, lastly, Louis-Philippe lived there.

The Petit Trianon

In 1761, Gabriel built a small square château, each façade of which was decorated differently, the richest being that with the tall Corinthian columns overlooking the French Garden. The inte-rior panelling dates from the time of Louis XV, apart from in the Mechanical Mirror Room created for Marie-Antoinette. The Petit Trianon was in effect a gift to Marie-Antoinette from Louis XVI on his accession to the throne. The Queen then transformed the garden and had the rare plants transferred to the King's Garden in Paris (Jardin des Plantes). She asked the architect Mique and the painter Hubert Robert to design an English Garden in its place: hence the appearance of small brooks, picturesque views and lawns.

Marie-Antoinette holding a rose, painted by Madame Vigée-Lebrun

This is undoubtedly the most famous portrait of the Queen, painted by her favourite artist. The wife of the Sovereign is depicted making a bouquet of roses, most probably in her garden at Trianon.

In 1777, Mique built the Rock Pavilion and the small mock-antique temple, known as the Temple of Love. In 1780, the small theatre was built, in which Marie-Antoinette deigned to appear and thus ensure the success of Beaumarchais' *Marriage of Figaro.*

The Queen's Hamlet

It was the Queen's Hamlet that made Marie-Antoinette's garden famous. Like Madame de Lamballe at Rambouillet and the Condés at Chantilly, Marie-Antoinette wanted a village of her own, whose houses, modelled on the style of Normandy cottages, would in fact be very elegant inside. Between 1783 and 1785 Mique built twelve houses, of which ten still stand, among them the Queen's Cottage, the Billiard Room, the Mill, the Boudoir, and the Pigeon Loft.

Mique had designed a tower joined to the Dairy by a small gallery. One used to be able to climb to the top via an outside staircase which no longer exists. From the top of the tower, one could fish with a line in the adjacent pond, hence its name the Fishery Tower. However, it was more often called the Marlborough Tower, after the song made famous by Madame Poitrine, the Dauphin's nurse.

VERSAILLES

Louis XIII
(1601-1643)

Anne of Austria
(1601-1666)

Louis XIV
(1638-1715)

Maria-Theresa
of Spain
(1638-1683)

Louis, Dauphin
(1661-1711)

Louis-François
(1672-1672)

Philippe-Charles
(1668-1671)

Marie-Thérèse
(1667-1672)

Marie-Anne
(1664-1664)

Anne-Elisabeth
(1662-1662)

Louis, duc
de Bourgogne
(1682-1712)

Philippe,
duc d'Anjou,
became Philip V
of Spain in 1700
(1683-1746)

Charles,
duc de Berry
(1686-1714)

1624
Louis XIII has a
hunting-lodge
built at Versailles.

1631
Louis XIII asks
Philibert Le Roy to build
a château on the site
of the hunting-lodge.

1643
Louis XIII stays at Versailles
for the last time.

1660
Marriage of Louis XIV
to Maria-Theresa of Spain.
The King brings his wife
to Versailles on October 25.

1664
Festivities of
Les Plaisirs de l'île enchantée.

1668
Grand Divertissement
at Versailles.

1682
Louis XIV declares Versailles
the official residence of the Court
and seat of government.

1684
Completion of
the Hall of Mirrors.

1710
Consecration of
the Royal Chapel on June 5.

1715
September 1, death of Louis XIV.
September 9, Louis XV abandons
Versailles for Vincennes.

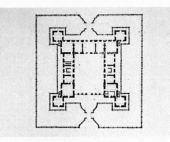

Louis XIII's "little château"

The Château of Versailles in 1668
by Pierre Patel

The colonnade (construction started in 1685)
by Jules Hardouin-Mansart

ENGLAND AND THE USA

1625
Charles I is proclaimed king
of England.

1649
Charles I is beheaded.

1653
Oliver Cromwell
is proclaimed Lord Protector.

1658
Death of Cromwell.
The Monarchy is restored.

1660
Charles II, raised to
the Court of Louis XIV,
rises to the throne

1666
Fire of London.

1682
The Sieur de la Salle founds
Louisiana.

1688
James II escapes to France.

1713
Treaty of Utrecht, Spanish
possessions are divided:
Philip V, grandson of Louis XIV,
keeps Spain and its colonies,
Britain gains Gibraltar, Minorca,
Newfoundland, Nova Scotia,
and the Hudson Bay territories.

1714-1727
Reign of George I.

Louis XV
(1710-1774)

Maria Leczinska
(1703-1768)

1722
Louis XV returns to live
at Versailles.

1736
September 26, opening of
the Hercules Drawing-Room.

1757
Attempt on Louis XV's
life by Damiens.

1768
The Petit Trianon
is completed.

1774
May 10, Louis XV dies of
smallpox at Versailles.

Louis Dauphin
(1729-1765)

Philippe-Louis
(1730-1733)

Adélaïde
(1732-1800)

Victoire
(1733-1799)

Sophie
(1734-1782)

Thérèse-Félicité
(1736-1744)

Louise
(1737-1787)

Louis XVI
(1754-1793)

Marie-Antoinette
of Austria-Lorraine
(1755-1793)

1777
Visit of Joseph II, Emperor
of Austria, the Queen's brother.

1783
Signing of the Treaty
of Versailles, acknowledging
the independence of
the United States of America.

1783-1786
Construction of
the Queen's Hamlet.

1789
May 5, opening of the States
General. October 6, the King,
the Royal Family and the Court
leave Versailles for good.

Louis-Philippe
(1773-1850)

1837
June 10,
Louis-Philippe
inaugurates the
museum dedicated
to the glories
of France.

Château of Versailles in 1722
by Pierre-Denis Martin

Illumination of the Belvedere in honour of Joseph II
by Claude-Louis Chatelet

Inauguration of the Hall of Battles
by Jean-Augusta Bard

1714-1727
Reign of George I.

1727-1760
Reign of George II.

1760-1820
Reign of George III.

1775-1783
The uprising in the American
colonies leads to recognition
of the United States

1777
The French General Lafayette
comes to fight alongside the
American insurgents.

1787
September 17,
United States Constitution.

1788
Creation of *The Times*.

1789
George Washington elected
President of the United States
of America.

1837
Queen Victoria
rises to the throne.

PHOTO CREDITS:
RMN/Lewandowski, RMN/Blot, Artephot/Varga,
Art Lys/Burnier, Art Lys/Girard, Art Lys/Néri, Art Lys/Février.

Achevé d'imprimer le 12 janvier 2000
Dépôt légal février 2000

Imprimé en CEE
Imprimé par Hérissey - Évreux (Eure) - N° 85927